# Mr. Mouthful

## and the Monkeynappers

**Joseph Kimble**

*illustrated by Kerry Bell*

*In memory of my mother, Marge,*
*and my sister, Karen.*

A reminder to all young readers:
You'll never be sorry if you learn to love words.



Hardcover: 978-1-7342097-5-4
Paperback: 978-1-7342097-4-7
Kindle: 978-1-7342097-6-1

Library of Congress Control Number and
Cataloging-in-Publication data on file with the publisher.

Book design and front-cover image: Kerry Bell
This is an original print edition of *Mr. Mouthful and the Monkeynappers*

Printed in the United States of America
10 9 8 7 6 5 4 3 2 1

Well, here comes Mr. Mouthful,
our favorite fancy-pants,
our fan of using big words.

He's out and about with Dupree,
who's sporting his brand-new shades
and some superlicious sneakers.

Pretty soon, young Lucy tags along,
and Jojo as well—in a line.

They're striding together as one,
left, right, left—all in step—
swaying from side to side,
raising their arms in the air.

They're having a blast.
They think it's a gas,
imitating that hotshot, Dupree.

Wait! There's an unmarked hole.
Mr. Mouthful, though, doesn't yell, "Stop!"
Instead, he bibblety-blathers:

Too late for the kids.
They fall in with a thud
and get covered with mud.

Mr. Mouthful was no help at all.

Two guys in a car are watching
as he and Dupree sashay on.
Then all of a sudden, Whoa!
Mr. Mouthful sings out loud.

"Disport, disport.
Strut your stuff."

And Dupree? He starts to dance.

He's doing the monkey.
He's jammin'; he's funky.
He's as bad as he can be.

Two kids are loving this scene.
Desmond and Molly join in,
matching the moves of Dupree.

But they don't see the bucket of paint.

Mr. Mouthful blurts,
"Urgent advisory: Dispense with the dancing forthwith."
They don't understand. Desmond trips on the can.
And Molly slides into the paint.

"A most unfortunate outcome,"

intones our incorrigible gasbag.

"We shall proceed
nonetheless."

They arrive at a soccer field,
where two teams are playing a game,
running and kicking like crazy.

They're pounding that ball
and giving their all,
when something amazing unfolds.

Tie game—and close to the end.
One side dribbles and passes downfield,
from Rita to Rocky to Jude,
who's headed full tilt toward the goal.

Gadzooks! Dupree dashes out,
dives in, and picks up the ball.
Then he runs back upfield.
He dodges and squeals.
He's a monkey who's on the loose.

Some kids fall down, giggling;
others run but can't catch him.

He sprints to a basketball court
and shimmies to the top of the pole.
He leaps in the air
with stupendous flair
and slam-dunks the soccer ball.

Mr. Mouthful has grabbed a stray bike.
He's pedaling in hot pursuit.
So are Rita and Rocky and Jude;
they're pumping as hard as they can.

Jude hits a stump
and goes down with a flump,

right into a pile of goose poo.

Then . . . a shocking turn of events.
As Dupree lopes onto the roadway,
those guys in the car hit the gas
and suddenly cut him off.

What do they want with Dupree?
Will they sell him or make him do tricks?
Dupree squeals and fights
with all of his might,
but they're hauling him off toward the car!

By now, though, the kids have caught up,
Rita and Rocky and lots more—
a posse to rescue Dupree.
Mr. Mouthful is not far behind.
He's screaming,

while Dupree is all in a panic.
He'll be locked in a cage.
He won't get to play.
He'll never be happy again.

Mr. Mouthful is going berserk:

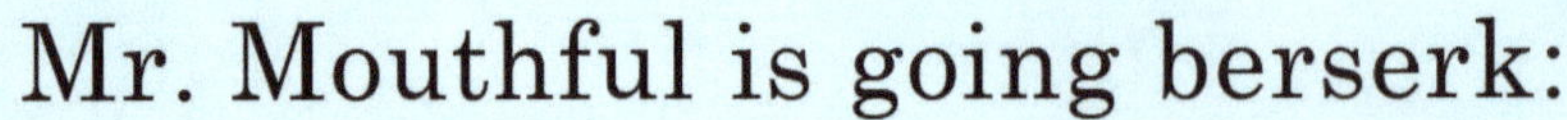

"*Unhand him, unhand him, you scoundrels,
or I'll have to summon the law.*"

But the kids—they swing into action.
They head in full force toward the men,
armed with juice boxes and fruit.

They let the things fly
and pelt the two guys,
who duck and let go of Dupree.

Meanwhile, there's an ear-splitting noise.
Rita blew her safety whistle!
That scares the pants off the guys.

As they're starting to motor away,
the kids fling more fruit—and some shoes—
and the car crashes into a ditch.

The youth brigade
has saved the day
and foiled the monkeynappers.

Then Rita and Rocky rush in.
Dupree is a little bit dazed,
so they each loop under an arm
and carry him—quickly—away.

Mr. Mouthful bikes to their side,
where he finally gets hold of himself.

He calls 9-1-1,
and soon the police come
and haul the two brutes off to jail.

Mr. Mouthful now turns to the kids,
who have gathered around in a group.
Will he chatter and jabber away?
Deliver a long-winded speech?

Maybe not, not this time.
Our guy is a little choked up.
With a tip of his hat,
he speaks simply at last:

Joseph Kimble is a distinguished professor emeritus at Cooley Law School, where he taught legal writing for 35 years. He has won several national and international awards for his work in promoting plain language in public communication.

Kerry Bell is a Canadian who likes to draw silly things. That usually means unimpressed cats and dancing people. She studied animation at the Emily Carr Institute in Vancouver, and lives in Mississippi with her husband and three impressive cats.

www.MrMouthful.com